THE SCIENCE OF SCIENCE

THIS IS A BOOK THAT COVERS THE MOST INTERESTING AND IMPORTANT TOPICS OF CLASS 6,7,8,9. IT IS ALMOST ESSENTIAL FOR STUDENT IN THESE CLASSES. IT IS ALSO JUST A FUN READ AS IT IS VERY INFORMATIVE AS WELL

AF408126

DHRUV GULATI

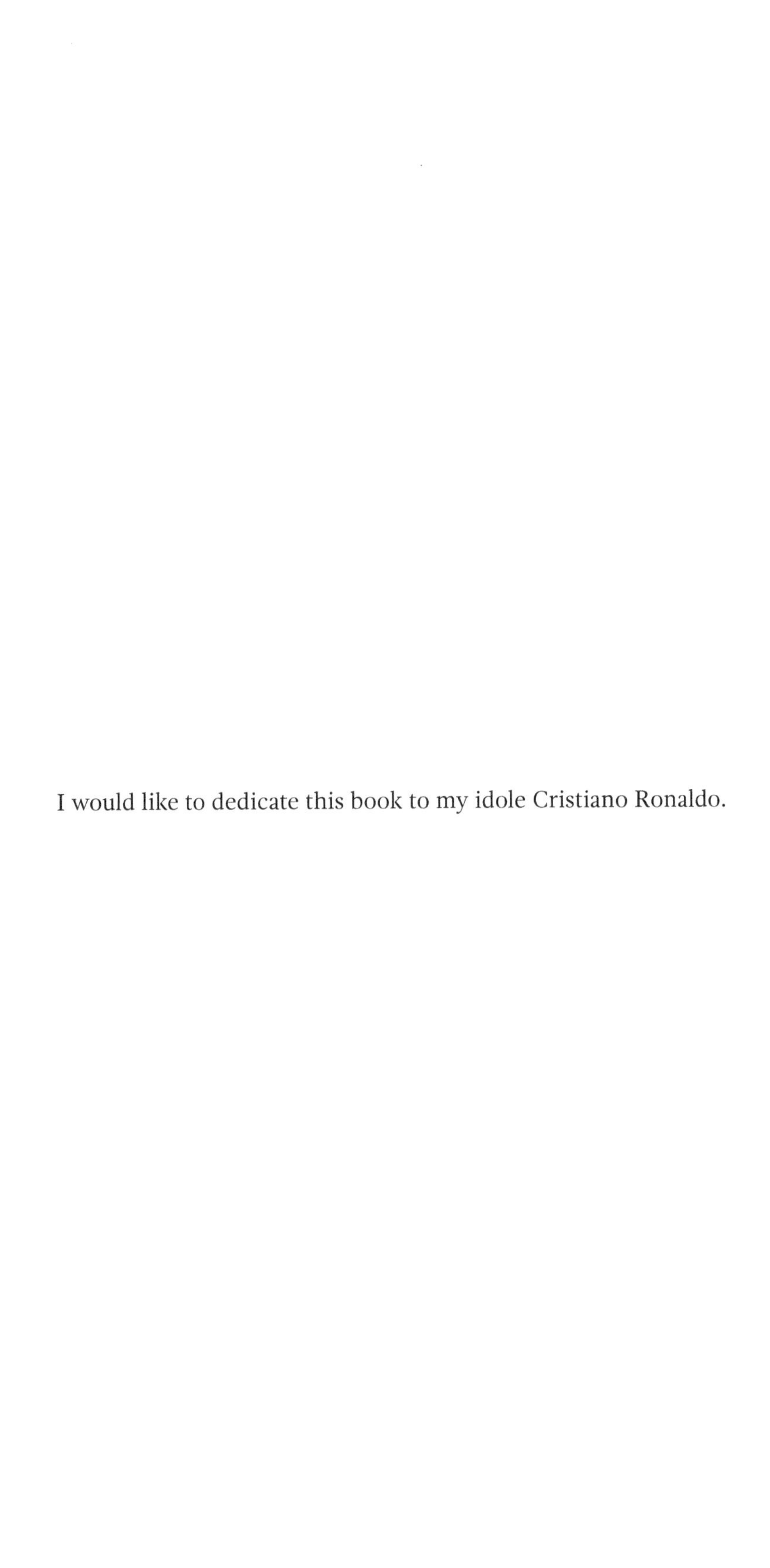

I would like to dedicate this book to my idole Cristiano Ronaldo.

Contents

Physics

Content

CHAPTER ONE

PLANETS

These are celestial bodies in space that resemble starts but they do not have their own light. They just reflect the sunlight falling on them.

They revolve around the Sun in a definite path called as orbit. The time taken to one revolution around the sun is called its period of revolution. This period increases as the distance of the planet increases from the Sun. So, Mercury has the shortest period of revolution whereas Neptune has the highest period of revolution. They have thier own gravity and they are smaller than stars.

A photo of the solar system that shows the different planets, their orbits and thier ditance away from the sun

All the planets are found in the solar system. A collection of solar system makes a galaxy and we are in the milky way galaxy. the closest galaxy to us is called Canis Major Dwarf galaxy. It is about 236000000000000000 km or 25000 light years away from the sun.

Murcury

It is the nearest planet to the Sun. It is the smallest planet of the solar system. It is not always visible from Earth, most of the time it remains hidden in Sun's glare. Sometimes it can be seen as a bright spot of light near the sun before sunrise and after sunset . Life is not possible on mercury due to high temperature, lack of water and atmosphere. Time period of revolution is 88 days and Time period of rotation is 59 days. It does not have any natural satellite of its own.

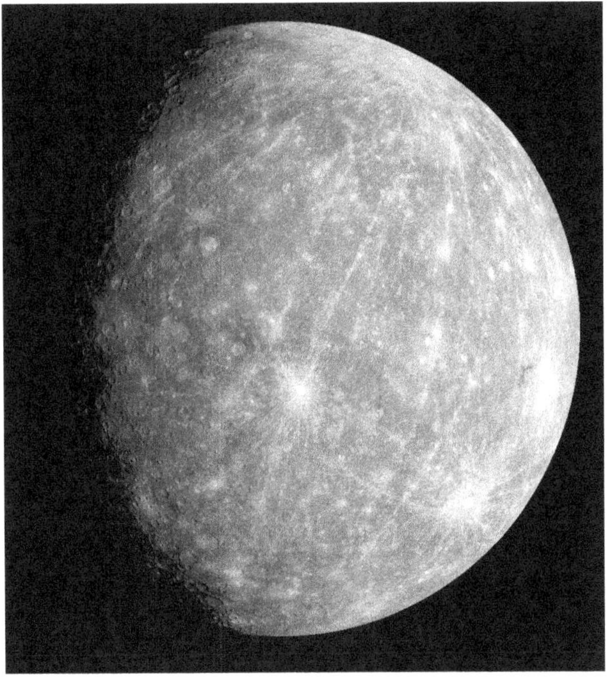

Mercury

Venus

It is the nearest planet to the Earth. It is called the shining planet or it is the brightest planet because it reflects almost all the light falling on its surface. This planet rotates from east to west. Time period of revolution is 225 days whereas time period of rotation is 116 days. It is the hottest planet in our solar system. Life is not possible on this planet as the atmosphere is made up of mainly carbon dioxide gas and has clouds of sulphuric acid meaning it traps a lot of the heat making it the hottest planet. It does not have any satellite. It is named after a God of beauty and love. It is the brightest planet of our solar system.

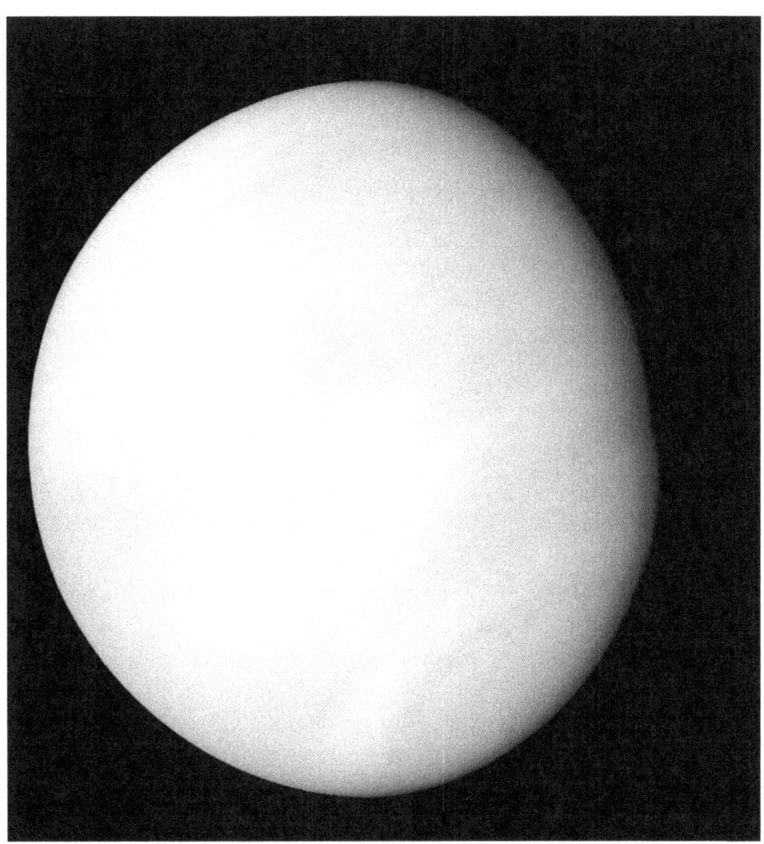

Earth

This is a unique planet as it supports life. Some reasons it supports life are:

~It has a perfect atmosphere as it has 78%of nitrogen, 21%of oxygen and 1% of other gases

~It has sufficient water as 70% of the Earth's surface is covered by water.

~There is presence of the ozone layer and this protects us from the harmful UV radiations of the Sun.

~Time period of revolution is 365 days and 6 hours.

~Time period of rotation is 24 hours.

~It has one natural satellite called moon.

Our beloved planet Earth

Mars

The planet next to the Earth is mars. It is visible for the greater part of a year. It looks reddish in color because the soil of mars contains iron in greater quantity. This is the reason why it is called Red planet. Time period of revolution around the sun is 67 days and the time period of rotation is 1.026 Earth days. It has two natural satellites called Phobos and Deimos. Its is named after the roman god of war. A day on Mars lasts 24 hours and 37 minutes.

Mars

Jupiter

It is the largest and the heaviest planet of the solar system. It is so large that it can occupy 1300 Earths in it. The mass of Jupiter is 318 times the mass of the Earth.

~Time period of revolution = 4333 days

~Time period of rotation = 9 hours and 55 minutes

~It has 67 moons till date

~Along with the moons it also has a faint ring its Equatorial plane.

Jupiter

Saturn

It is the second largest planet of the solar system. It is called the ringed planet because it has several rings round it, these rings are made up of ice as dust particles revolving around the planet. This planet is least dense among all. It has 62 moons.

Time period of revolution = 29.45 Earth years

Time period of rotation = 10 hours and 39 minutes

Saturn

Uranus

It is the third largest planet of the solar system. It has greenish appearance because of the presence of ammonia and methane clouds in the atmosphere. It has 27 moons. Like Venus this planet rotates from east to west. Time period of revolution is 84 years and the time period of rotation is 0.78 days.

It has highly tilted rotational axis. Hence, it appears to roll by its side.

Uranus

Neptune

It is the fourth largest planet of the solar system. It is the planet furthest from the Sun. It has 13 natural satellites. The time period of revolution is 165 years and the time period of rotation is 16 hours and 7 minutes. It is the coldest planet.

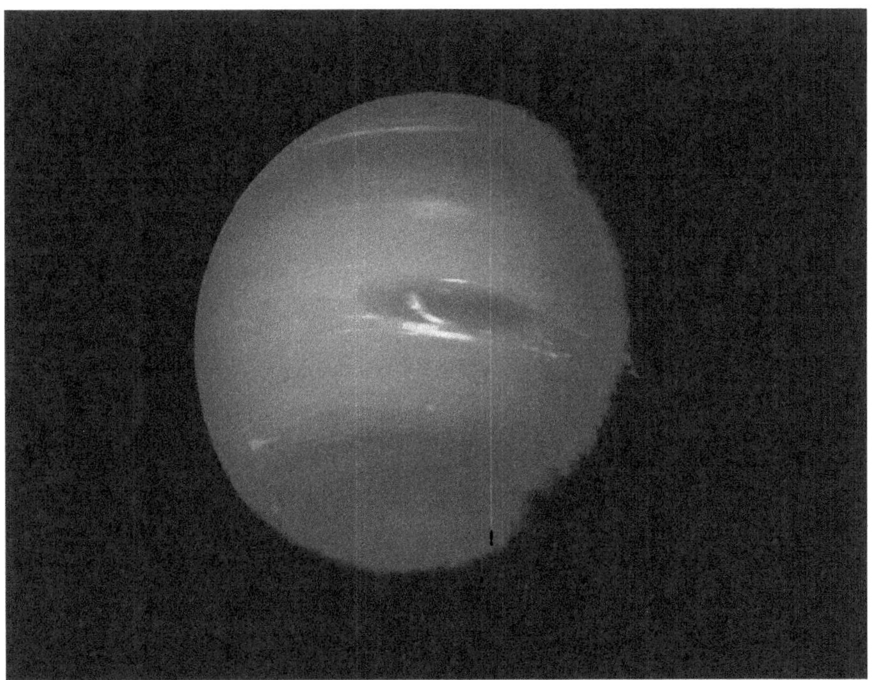

Neptune

CHAPTER TWO

OTHER THINGS IN OUR SOLAR SYSTEM

There are many other things in our solar system apart from the planets:

1. Asteroids - The small irregular peices of rocks and metal that revolve around the sun in between the orbits of mars and jupiter are called asteroids. They have their own orbit around the sun .There are almost 1.1 million asteriods in the asteroids belt. They are of various sizes as the largest one is hundrads of kilometers in diameter and the smallest one is about 100 km. Sometimes these asteroids colid with each other while orbiting and this gives rise to sooting stars.

2. Comets - A comet is a small body made up of ice and dust that revolves in highly elongated orbits around the sun. They revolve the sun in a very elliptical orbit and the period of revolution around the sun is usually very long. It apperas as a bright head with a tail. the head consistes of ice, dust and rocks. As the comet approaces the sun its tail increase as when the comet approaches the sun the gases, dust particles and water vapours in the tail get pushed away by the pressure of the solar rediations. the most famous comet is the Halley`s comet as it is only seen once every 76 years. It was last seen in 1986 and the next time it will be seen is in 2026.

3. Meterodis- These are the bodies present in our solar system that can range a lot in size. They could be as small as a grain of sand or as large as

a boulder. they orbit the sun and are spread out all over the solar system unlike the asteriods.

4. Meteros- If a meteroid losses its orbit and enters the Earth`s atmosphere it is known as a meteros. So a meteroids are the bodies that we can see as a bright streak of light that flashes for a moment across the sky. Meteros are also called shooting stars. When a metero enters into the atmosphere of the Earth with high speed a lot of heat is produced due to the resistance of the air. THis heat results in the burning of the metero which can be seen as a streak of light shooting down from the sky. It falls on Earth in the form of dust.

5. Meteroids- When the metero is big then a part of it may not get burned up in the air and when a metero does not burn completely while entering the atmosphere of the Earth then it is called a meteroid. They are made up of rock or metal. More than 3000 meteroids fall on Earth each year in different parts of the Earth. Meteroids are believed to be formed at the same time as the planets of the solar system and so by studying the compositions of the meteroid scientists can get valuable information about the materials of which all the planets are made up of.

CHAPTER THREE

LIGHT

Light- It is a form of energy which produces the sensation of vision.

Properties of light:

1. Light dose not require any medium for its propogation it can travel through vaccum also.

2. Light always travels in a straight line and this motion of the light is called the rectinear motion

3. It has very high speed. I is 3*10 to the power of 8.

Impornant term related with light

1. Sources of light- Those objects which emit light of their own. They may be also be man-made. Example: Sun, stars and fireflys are natural sources whereas torch, candle and lamp are man made sources of light.

2. Luminous objects - Those objects which emit light of their own are called luminous objects. Example: Sun, stars and candle.

3. Hot source of ight- A source that emits both heat and light is called a hot source of light. Example: bulbs, sun, lamp, candles etc.

4. Cold source of light- A source that only emits light is called cold source of light. Example tube light and CFC bulb.

5. Incandesent objects- Objects that emit light when heated to a hogh temperature are called incandesent objects.

6. Non luminous object- Those objects which do not emit light but can reflect light but can reflect light are called non luminous objects. Examples: book, table, moon and mirror.

7. Transparent medium- Allow the light to pass through it completely is called transparent. Example glass.

8. Translucent medium- Allows a part of light to pass through it. Example oil paper.

9. Opaque medium- Does not allow any light to pass through it. Example brick, book, table etc.

Laws of reflection

~ The angle of incidence is always equal to the angle of refection

~ The incident ray, the reflected ray and the normal all lie on the same plane at the point of incidence.

Sunlight

The light coming from the sun is reffered to as white light but when this light is passed through a prism it spliits into 7 colours meaning white light is a mixture of 7 colours.

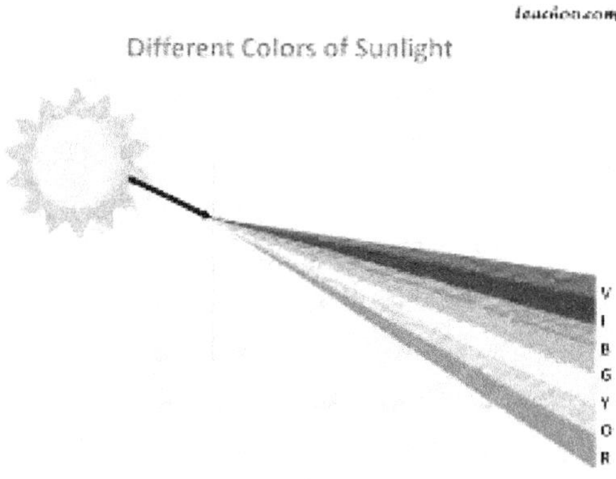

Sun light splitting into 7 colours when passed through a prism.

The 7 colours that white light splits into are:
1.Blue
2.Red
3.Green
4.Yellow

5.Indigo

6.Violet

7.Orange

Dispersion of light- The phenonmenon of spliting white light into its constituent 7 colours.

Rainbow- It is the optical phenoenon that is caused when tiny droplets of the rain acts as a small prism for the white light to split into 7 colours. The result is that these colours form a beautiful multicoloured arc.

Human eye

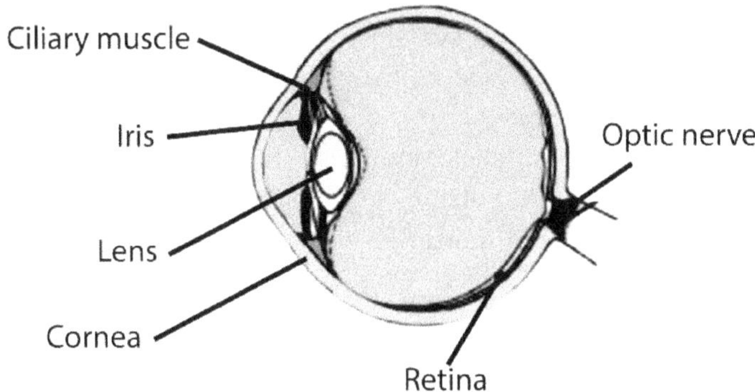

Human eye

Parts of the human eye:

1. Cornea- It is made up of the transparent tissue. It is the bulging part of the eye. It acts as a window to the world. Light enters he interior of the eye throug cornea.It remains moist and dust free due to the secretion from he tear glands.

2. Iris- It is a dark muscular diaphragm which is suspended behind cornea.

The tiny opening in the iris is pupil. The pupil appears black as all the light falling on it goes inside the eye.

The function of iris is to control the amount of light entering the eye, by changing the size of the pupil.

3. Crystalline lens- It is double convex lens made up of tranparent tissue. The function is to focus the light rays.

4. Retina- It acts like a screen where a image f the object is forned. It is formed by two cells.

Rod cells- They become ctive in dim light and their function is to sense the intensity of light.

Cones cell- They become active in bright light and their function is to sense the colour.

5. Optic nerve- It consits lots of nerve fibres and the function is to send optical signal to the brain.

6. Yellow spot- The reign of retina, which is moist sensitive to light also the reign where the sharpest image is formed.

7. Blind spot- The point where the optical nerve leaves the eye ball. It is also called the area of 0 vision.

8. Cillary muscels- A bundle of muscels, which keeps lens in its position. The function is to change the shape of cystalline lens so that it can focus on objects placed at different distance.

CHAPTER FOUR

EARTHQUAKES

An earthquake is a sudden shaking or tremblimg of earth`s crust which lasts for a very short time. It is due to sudden release of energy in the earth`s crust that creates seismic waves. The waves are recorded with a seismometers also known as seismograph. The magnitude of earthquake is measured on the richter scale. If the magnitude the earthquake is higher than a 7 on the richter scale, it causes serious damage very large areas. The largest earthquakes in history have been of magnitude slightly over 9 but there is no limit to a possible magnitude.

Causes of earthquakes
There are 3 main causes of eathquakes which are:
- Movement of earth`s plates
-Volcanic eruptions
-Anthropogenic factor

Movement of earth`s plates- The outermost layer of the earth is not in one piece, it is made up of a number of separate slabs or plates of rocks called tectonic plates. These plates float over semi molten magma and moves slowly and continously in geological scale of time. As these move sometimes they colide with each other. the vibrations produced from this collision are sent in shock waves in all directions. When these vibrations hit the surface of the earth they result in earthquakes. These are the most common types of earthquakes.

Volcanic eruption- It is the cause of earthquake which occurs due to explosion f hot gases. Such earthquakes occur either simultaneously with erption or in the period preceding the eruption. They are caused by a sudden violent displacement of lava within the volcano. Their area of disturbance is quite small but their intensity can be huge especially near the volcano.

Anthropogenic factors- Humans also play a important role in the way nature works. Here are some actions taken by humans which can lead to earthquakes.

i. Underground mining- During underground mining the weight of all the rocks above the mines comes on only the walls and when these walls fail to support such a large weight, they collapes and this causes eartquakes.

ii. By blasting of rocks- When rocks are blasted off to build buildings, dams or roads this could cause earthquakes

iii. Nuclear explosions- nuclear testing explosions can cause very powerful seismic waves and these cause earthquakes.

vi. Dams and reserviors- The huge amount of water stored in one place can put a lot of pressure on the Earth below it and this could cause the tectionic plates to slide and cause earthquakes.

Consequences of Earthquakes:
- Building collape
- Land slide
- Fire
- Loss of life
- Loss of property
- Tsunamis
- Flash floods

Protection against earthquakes
- Building in seismic zones should so be disigned that they can withstant large tremors
- In the construction of buildings light material like timber or mud should be used.

- Make sure that the fan, coolers, shelfs, caupboards etc are fitted firmly.

What to do during an earthquake if you are indoors?
1. Take shelter under heavy objects.
2. Do not go to the other rooms, stay away from tall and heavy objects.
3. If you are in bed, do not get up just protect your head with a pillow.
4. If in a cinema hall or all do not use lift or escalators.
5. Shut off kitchen gas, do not light candles.

What to do during an earthquake if you are outdoors?
~ If inside a vehicle, drive slowly to an open area, stay away from tall buildinds, flyovers and heavy power trees.

CHAPTER FIVE

LIGHTNING

Lightning is an atmospheric discharge of electricty which comes with thunder and it usually occurs with thunderstom, duststom or volcanic eruption. There are about 1.4 billion lightning flashes in the world every year. In the atmospheric discharge of electricity the electricity can travel at speeds of 220000 km/h and he temperatures could even be 30000 degree celcius.

How does lightning take place?

During thunderstoms as the water droplets move downwards and the air current moves upwards this causes the charges to seperate. The positive charges move the upper part of the cloud and the negative charges move to the lower part of the cloud. Also there are positive charge present just above the surace of Earth and in this situation as the negitive charges near the lower part of cloud and the positive charges right above the surface of Earth attract each other, at that time the air which is usually a poor conderctor of electricity becomes a good conductor and allows these charges to meet. We see this as lightning. A single flash of lightning is called a lightning bolt.

Effects of lightning

Negative

1. It can cause loss of life and property.

2. As lightning has very high temperature, when it hits a tree it could cause the tree to explode.

3. It can cause forest fire.

Positive

1. It played a important role in the evolution of life on the Earth.

2. As light passes through the air it turns the oxygen into ozone and this is very important for the future of Earth.

What to do during lightning if you are outdoors?

1. Look for shelter: A bus, a car or a train is a good shelter because the metallic body of the vehicles act as a conducting path and the person inside the vehicle is safe.

2. If you are in a forest or park take shelter under a short tree but not a long one.

3. Stay away from swimming pools because water is a good conductor of electricity.

4. Do not use an umbrella, because it will act as a conducting path for lightning bolt.

5. In a group stay 15 feet away from each other.

6. In an open ground where there is no safe place where there is no safe place, squat low on the round with your hands on your knees and head between your hands.

What to do during lightning if you are indoors?

1. Stay away from electrical appliances like fridge, TV, iron etc but lights can remain on.

2. Do not use corded telephones. Although mobile phones and cordless phones can be used.

3. Stay away from door, windows, metallic pipes, electric wires.

CHAPTER SIX

FORCES

It is a pull or a push which arises due to the interaction between the objects. Its SI unti is Newton and is represented by N.

Causes of force: It arises because of the interaction between objects

Effects of force

1. A force can move a stationary object- Roll a pen on your table that was not moving before. It was not moving but when force was applied to it, it stared to move.

2. A force can stop a moving object- Throw a ball in the air, when it comes down catch it. The ball was moving towards the ground but when you applied force to it by catching it, it stoped moving.

3. A force can change the speed of a moving object- If your friend kicks a football towards you and you also kick the ball in the same direction it was going then the speed of the ball would increase as more force has been applied on it.

4. A force can change the direction of a moving object- If a friend throws a ball at you and you hit it in the opposite direction to where it was going then the ball would change its direction as a force was applied on it.

5. A force can the shape and size of an object- look at the shape and size of a sponge, then squeeze it between your hands, you will be able to see the shape and size change due to the application of force on the sponge.

Types of forces

There are 2 main types of force: contact forces and non contact forces.

CONTACT FORCET

These forces come into play only when the two objects interacting with each other are in physical contact. For example; Muscular force and frictional force.

Muscular force- The force exerted by the muscles of the body is called the musclar force. Both human beings and animals exert muscular force to do work. Humans use this force for everday tasks like: walking, running, pushing, pulling, jumping and etc. Animals use muscular forces for pulling carts like the horse or plouging like the ox or carrying havey logs like the elephant.

Examples of muscular force are- Lifting a book from a table
- Drawing a bucket of water from the well

Frictional force- It is a force, which comes into play when an object tends to move or actually moves over the surface of another object. Its direction is opposite to the relative motion of the object.

Examples of friction are- when we roll a ball on the ground and it stops after some time due to the friction between it and the ground.
- when we stop rowing a boat in water and its slows down and after sometime it comes to rest this is due to the friction between it and the surafce of water. This also shows that friction is also applied in fluids , it is called fluid friction or viscous drag.

NON CONTACT FORCE

Aforce which can come into play without any physical contact between the objects are called non contact forces. For example magnetic force, gravitational force and electrostatic force.

Magnetic force- The force exerted by a magnet on another magnet or a megnetic material like iron, nickel, cobalt, steel etc is called magnetic force.

This force can be repulsive as well as attractive as when 2 unlike poles are close to each other then they attract but when 2 like poles are close to each other they repell each other.

Examples of magnetic force- bringing a metal nail near a magnet
- bringing a magnet near another magnet

Gravitational force- Every object in this universe is attracted to every other object with a force, which is the gravitational force.

Properties of gravity- It dependes on the masses of the objects and the distance between their centres.

-This force is independent of the medium between the objects
-This force will bring the objects to move towards each other
-It is always attractive and it is same for both the object
-It is a long range force
-It is the weakest force in nature

Electrostatic force- It is a force exerted by a charged body on the other charged or unchared body. This force comes into play even when the bodies are not in contact.It is a stronger force than than the gravitational force.

CHAPTER SEVEN

FRICTION

What is friction?

It is a contact force which comes into play when an object tends to move or actually moves over another surface in contact.

Frictional force opposes the relative motion of two surfaces in contact. It acts on both the surface.

Factors affecting friction

1. Nature of the surfaces in contact- Irregularities give rise to friction. When we try to move one surface over another theese irregulatities are locked nto one another and some of the applied force is used to overcome these irregularities. A rough surface has more irregularities so friction is more. Hence, as the roughness of the surface increases friction also increases. A smooth suface has less irrgularities so friction is less. Hence, as the smoothness of the surface increases friction decreases.

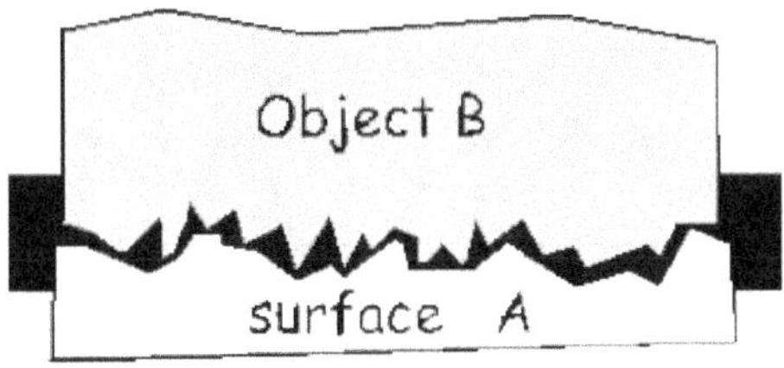

The irregularities that cause friction

2. Normal reaction- In the case of horizontal motion the normal reaction is equal to the weight of the object. The frictional force acting between an

object and a surface over which it moves or tends to move depends on the normal reaction of the object. This means that heavier the object more will be the force of friction.

3. Area of contact- The friction force acting between two objects is not affected by the area of contact between the two objects.

Static friction

When there is no applied force, thereis no applied force, there is no friction. Friction will come into play the moment there is an applied force.

The force of friction which comes into play between the two surfaces in contact before they start moving relative to each other is called static friction.

Maximum of the static riction is called limiting friction

Kinetic friction/ Sliding friction

The force of friction which comes into play when the two surfaces actually start moving relative to each other.

Kinetic friction is always more than static friction

Kinetic friction is less than the limiting friction because the contact points of one surface do not get enough time to lock with the contact points of the surface over which it slides.

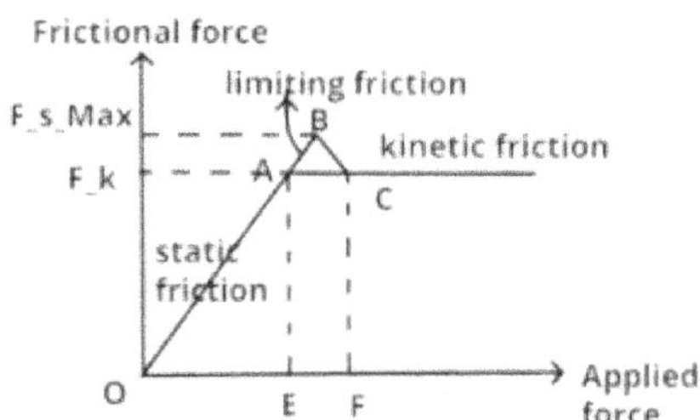

Graph that shows frictional force with respect to applied force

Rolling friction

When objects like wheel, sphere or cylinder move over a surface the friction that comes into play is rolling friction.

Cylinder takes less time to reach the bottom than the block. This implies that rolling is easier than sliding.

Hence, the friction in the case of rolling is less than the sliding friction. Wheels has been considered as the greatest invention of mankind because rolling friction is less than sliding friction and heavy loads can be pull from one place to the other easily by placing them on carts with wheels.

In factories as far as possible sliding friction is converted into the rolling friction by the use of wheels and ball bearing.

Advantages of friction

1. Friction helps us to hold the things firmly.

2. It helps us to run and walk

3. Vehicles move on the road because of the friction between the tyres and the road.

4. We are able to sit on a chair because of friction between the chair and us.

5. We are able to write on paper and board due to friction.

6. A match stick lights due to friction when we rub the head of the match stick to the rough surface of match box, the temperature of the match stick rises to the ignition temperature hence, the chemicals in the match stick catches fire, which lights the match stick.

Disadvantages of friction

1. Loss of energy is there because anything that is moving it has to overcome friction.

2. The moving parts of machines produce heat due to friction, hich results in the wasteage of energy.

3. The tyers of vehicles and soles of shoes wear out in few month because of the force of friction.

As energy is wasted in overcoming friction but it is required for walking, running and holding the things so we can say that it is a neccessary evil.

Ways to increase friction
- Increasing the roughness of the surfaces in contact.
- Increasing the normal reaction.

Ways to decrease friction
- By polishing the surfaces to make them smooth.
- By appling lubricants to reduce friction. Lubricants and the substances like: oil or grease these substances to form a ayer over the surface which reduces the irregularities, between the surfaces and the surface do not come in direct contact because of this layer of lubricants.
- By using ball bearing because it will convert the slidding friction to rolling friction.
- By giving the body a streamlined shape, friction can be reduced.

Biology

Content

CHAPTER EIGHT

CELL

Cells are the basic structural and functional unit of all life forms. All living forms are composed of microscopic unit called cell. The study of structure and composition of cell is called 'Cytology.' Cell was first discovered and observed by Rbert Hooke in a thin dead slice of cork in the year 1665. First free living cell was discovered by A.V.Leeuwenhoek in 1674.

Cell theory

It was a theory about cell and it was given by 2 biologists called Schleiden and Schwann in 1674. The teory was:

1. All plants and animals are composed of cell.
2. Cell is the basic unit of life.
3. All cells arise from pre-existing cell.

Viruses are an exeption to this theory.

Cell shape- Cells are of many different sizes and shapes for example cells can be spherical like the WBC also they may be elongated like nerve cells.

Cell size

- The largest cell is the ostrich egg.
- The longest cell is the nerve cell.
- The smallest cell is known as PPLO mycoplasma.

Parts of cell

Cell membrane- It is selectively permeable in nature meaning it allows some substance to pass through it but not all can.

- It is made up of protein and lipids (which are made up of fats and oils.)

- It is flexible in nature due to this the air spaces between the lipids and protein as if we apply force these spaces compress and return to there original shape.

- Its function is to protect the inner organelles of the cell. It also regulates what moves in and out of the cell

Osmosis- It is the process by which water can go in and out of the plasma membrane. It is the process by which water and other solvent move in and out of a semipermeable membrane like the plasma membane. There are two main types of osmosis:

1. Endomosis

2. Exosmosis

Endomosis- Movement of solvent into the cell is called as endomosis. This solution is also also called hypertonic solution.

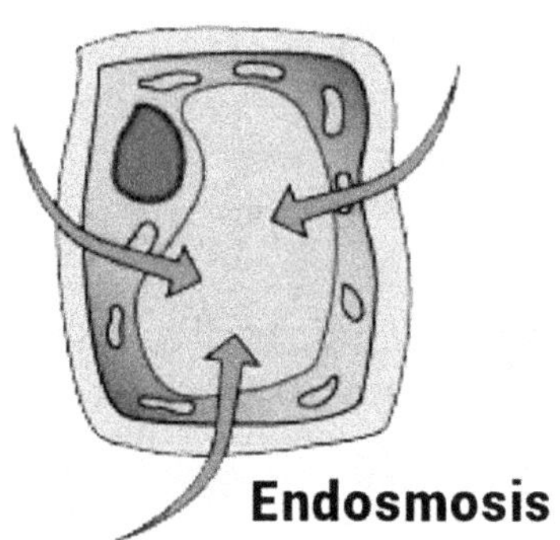

Exosmosis- The movement of solvent outside the cell is called as Exosmosis. This solution is also called Hypotonic.

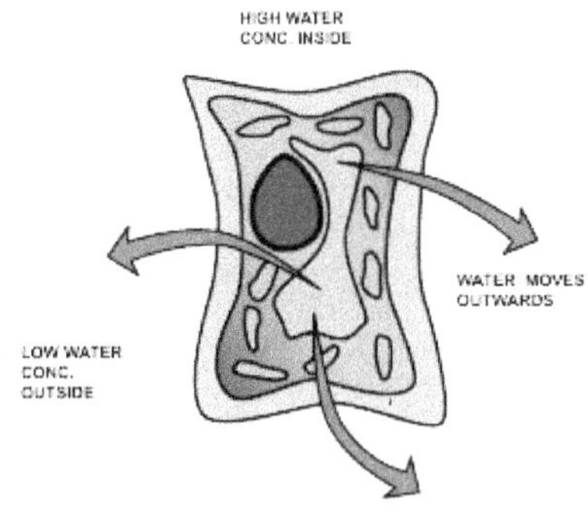

Cell wall- It is the outermost layer of the plant cell. It is not present in animal cells

- It is a rigid, strong, thick porous and non living structure.

- It is non living as it is made up of a chemical and that is not living.

Q. Why is cell wall absent in animal cell but present is plant cell?

Ans. Plant cell can not move during natural phenomenon like rain, storm etc but animals can move. So cell wall is present there to provide plant cell an extra layer of potection.

What are the function of cell wall?

1. It provides shapes to the cell.

2. It provides strenght to the cell.

3. It is highly permeable and allows many molecules inside the cell.

Nucleus- It has a membrane bound, which is called nuclear membrane. It has a double layered covering.

- It was first discovered in 1831 by Robert Brown.

- It is called the controle tower, brain and the headquarter of the cell.

- In Prokaryotes it is called nucleoid as it is not well defined unlike in eukaryotes.

- All the genetic material is stored within the nucleus as DNA and it is stored in the chromatin part of the nucleus. Chromatin is made up of DNA and protein.

- Nucleus has many nuclear pores which helps with nucleus going in and out of it.

- It also has a jelly like liquid in it called nucleoplast.

CHAPTER NINE

DIFFERENCE BETWEEN PLANTS CELL AND ANIMAL CELL

Plant cell

- Stores food in the form of starch.
- Contains chloroplast for photosynthesis.
- Have a cell wall to maintain structure and rigidity.
- Usually does not contain lysosomes and peroxisomes.
- Cells are square and rigod or geometric shaped.
- Limited movement.
- Have one large central vacuole.
- Cytoplasm is fusted to periphery by vacuole.

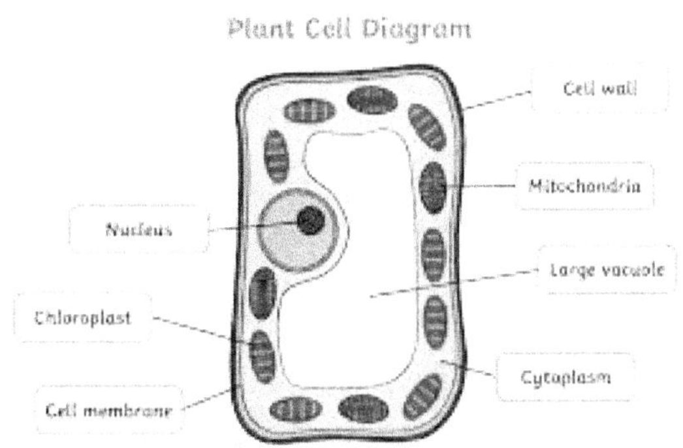

Plant cell diagram

Animal cells

- Sortes food in the form of glucose or glucogen.
- No cell wall.
- Contains cilia or flagella.
- Cells are fluid and flexible, many shapes.
- Cells can move around.
- Has small or no vacuole.
- Cytoplasm fills the entire cell.

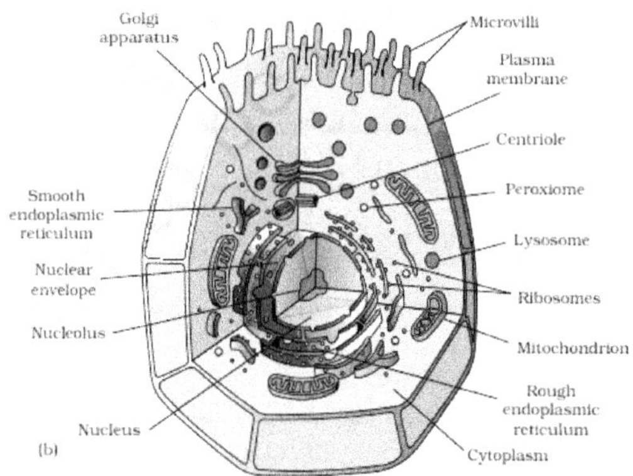

Animal cell diagram

CHAPTER TEN

AIR POLLUTION

What is air?

Air is the mixture of different gases. It is made up of 78 percent of nitrogen. 21 percent of oxygen. 0.93 percent of argon. 0.03 percent of carbon dioxide

What is pollution?

It is the undesirable change in the physical, chemical and bological properties of air, water and land.

What is air pollution?

It is the contamination of air by unwanted substances which have harmful effects on biotic and abiotic component of biosphere.

What are its causes?

There are two types of causes for air pollution: natural and those caused by Humans.

Natural causes: -Volcanic eruption

-Pores

-Forest fires

-Pollen grains

-Dust storm

Caused by humans: -Exhaust of automobiles- 60-80 percent of air pollution and 75 percent of noise pollution is due to this

-Factories

-Fire wood

-Dung cake

Now we will be explaining some air pollutents, their sources, their effect on plants and animals

1. Pollutent- carbon monoxide(CO)

Sources- In complete combustion of fossil fuel

- Ciggratte smoke

Effects- The job of RBCs is to carry the oxygen to the diffent parts of the body but cabon monoxide sticks to the RBCs and this causes a lack of oxygen in many parts of the body. This can leaaad to death in as low as 30 mins due to the lack of oxygen.

2. Pollutent- Sulphur dioxide (SO2)

Souces- In complete combustion of fossil fuels

Effects on plants- Decreases photosynthesis

- Lichens are sensitive of SO2

- It changes he structure of chlorophyll

- Decreased growth

Effects on animals- Eye irritation

- Respiratory problems

When sulphur dioxide is added to water it results in sulphuric acid

Sulphuric acid causes acid rain that distroys crops, burns holes in leaves of plants, decreass the number of fish in water and removes basic nutrients such as calcium from the soil.

3. Pollutent- Nitrogen oxides (NOx)

Sources- Incomplete combustioon of fossil fules

Effects on plants- It distroys the necrosis tissue

Effects on animals- Eye irritation

- Throat, nose injury

4. Pollutent- Methan

Sources- Marshy areas

Effects- it is a green house gas therefore it causes global warming

5. Pollutent- Formaldehyde
    Sources- newly formed carpets
    Effects- Cancer

GHG (Green house gases)
    - Trap infra red radiation
    - Re radiate them to the earth`s surface
    - Earth remains warm this is due to the green house effect
    - Annual mean temperature of Earth is 15 degress celcius
    Green house effect- It is the phenomenon of keeping the earth warm by the presence of green house gases in the atmasphere
    Green house gases- Carban dioxide(CO2), methane(CH4), nitrous oxide(N2O), chloro floro carbons(CFC)
    Global warming- Rise in annal mean temperature of earth due to enhanced green house effect is called global warming.
    Effects of global warming- rise in sea levels
    - effects the rainfall patteren
    - increase droughts

CHAPTER ELEVEN

Micro Organisms

They are the living organisms which cannot be seen by the naked eye but only be obsered under a microscope.

They are present everywhere and make up almost 50% of the weight of all linving organisms on Earth.

The part of science about micro organisms is called micro biology.

There are 5 main classification of micro organisms

- Fungi
- Bacteria
- Protozoa
- Alga
- Virus

Diseses caused by viruses

1. Cold
2. Cough
3. Hapatitis
4. Influenza
5. Chicken pox
6. Polio
7. AIDs

Habitats of micro organisms

They can be present in:

- Soil
- Air
- Water
- Plant
- Animals

They can even be present in extreme conditions like:

- Saline water
- Hot water spring
- Desert
- Marshy area
- Ice cold water
- Strong acid

Archebacteria- These are the types of bacteria that can survive in extreme conditions.

Micro organims positive and negitive sides
Positives

- Used in food production.
- Used in the production of alcohol, wine and acetic acid.
- Used in the produccction of antibiotics.
- Used in the production of vaccines.
- They clean the evironment.
- They increase soil fertility.

Negitives

- They cause diseases in animals, plants and humans.
- They can cause food poisoning.

Food production for micro organisms

1. Product- curd

    Micro organisms- LAB (Lactic acid bacteria)
    Caused by- Bacteria
    Process- Lactose turns into Lactic acid. This happens due to partial digestion of protein in milk.
    2. Product- Bread
    Microbes- Yeast. Yeast used for baking is called beaker's yeast.
    Caused by- Fungi
    Process- Alcoholic fermentation is done by yeast- breaking down food into acohol, CO2 and energy. So, when we put yeast in the dough of bread containg warm water, sugar and flour. Then yeast reproduhces rapidly. While respiring the CO2 fill the dough increasing its volume and make it into bread.

Vaccine
    What is a vaccine? How dose it work?
    Dead or weakened pathogens are injected in the body, antibiotics develope and kill the pathogen and remembers the mechanisms. So when actual infection occurs, antibodies remain and protect us from the disease.
    Immunity- It is the state of having sufficient biological defence to avoid infections.
    Vaccines are given for infection such as:

1. Cholera
2. Tuberculosis
3. Small pox
4. Hapatitis
5. Polio

Diseases- they are of 2 main types communicable and non communicable diseases
    Communicable disease-They are the disease that can spread from an infected person to a healthy person via food, water, air and physical contact. For example:

- Tuerclosis
- Typhoid
- Chicken pox
- Cholera
- Common cold

Non communicable disease- They are the disease that can not spread from an infected person to a healthy person. For example:

- Cancer
- Rickets
- Night blindness
- Cystitis
- Kwashiorkor

Food poisoning- Not properly preserved food leads to the growth of microorganism which leaves poisonous toxins. When we eat this food, these toxin enter our blood casuing nausea, vomitting and diarria.

Food preservation

1. Chemicals- vinegar, sodium benzoate, sodium metabisulphite. Jam, Jelly, Sauce, Squash
2. Salt: Meat, fish, pickels
3. Sugar: It reduces moisture and prevents the food from going bad. Jam, Jelly, Squash
4. Dehydration: Papads, Vegetable
5. Oil: Pickels, Meat, Fish, Vegetable, Fruits
6. Pasteruisation: Invented by Louis Pasteur for prevention of the soilage of milk. To do this milk is heated for abou 30 seconds and then chilled suddenly after.
7. Sterlisation- Heating at high temperature(150 degree celcius) with steam.
8. Refrigeration- Low temperature prevents the food.
9. Storage and packing- Air tight containers prevent the growth of microbes.

Chemistry

Content

CHAPTER TWELVE

ELECTRO PLATING

What is electro plating?

The process of deposition a layer of any desired metal on the other metal by means of electicity is called electroplating

Process of electroplating

- The metal to be electroplating is made up by the cathode (connected to th negitive terminal of the battery)
- The metal which is to be deposited on the anode (connected to the positive terminal of the battery)
- Salt solution of the metal to be deposited is tsaken as electrolyte.

Uses of electolysis

1. Electroplating - Tin cans which are made to store food by electroplating tin onto Iron. Tin is less reactive than iron. So, food do not come in contact with the iron directly. Hence, it is protected from getting spoited. Chromiun electroplaitng is on objects because it has entry appearence it does not corrode and resist scratches.
2. It is used in the extraction of the metals from their ores.
3. To seprate metals form impure metals

CHAPTER THIRTEEN

COAL

Physical properties of coal

- It is a fossile fuel
- There are black in colour
- It looks hard
- They are porous and hard
- Its main element is carbon
- It is used as a great source of energy
- It is very combustible

Formation: Coal was formed by decomposition of dead plants and trees (dead vegetation) into carbon. This takes about 300 million years that is why it is such a scarce resource. Due to high temperature and pressure inside the earth`s crust, and the due to no air inside the earth, the dead plants and trees got slowly converted into coal. For the formation of coal:

- Time
- High pressure
- High temperature
- Absence of air

Is very important. Slowly after time these plants and animals decay away but the energy dose not and this gets stored in the form of coal this process is called carbonization.

Constituents of coal

1. Coke- It is the purest form of carbon. It is very dark in colour, it is quite hard and solid. It is dence and quite porous. It is mixed with iron to make steel also it is used for the extraction of many metals from their ores.
2. Coal tar- Coal tar is a mixture of different carbon compounds. It thick, black liquid with unpleasant smell. The fractional distillation of coal tar gives many chemical substances which are used in the preparation of dyes, explosives, paints, synthetics fibers, drugs, and pesticides. One of the most important thing made from coal tar is naphthalene balls and they are used to repel insects and moths. It is a mixture of more than 200 substances.
3. Coal gas- Coal gas is obtained during the processing of coal to get coke. It is a mixture of hydrocarbons and carbon monoxide. It is used as a fuel in many industries situated near the coal processing plants. Coal gas was used for street lighting for the first time in London in 1810 and in New York around 1820. Now a days, it is used as a source of heat rather than light. It is used as a fuel in many industries.

Uses of coal

- Coal is used as fuel to heat boilers and ovens.
- Coal is the largest source of energy for the generation of electricity worldwide.
- Coal is one of the important fuel used to cook food in rural areas.
- Coal burns with a smokeless flame and therefore considered as a better domestic fuel.
- Coal is used for the extraction of metal from thier ores.
- Coal is an ssential raw material for steel industry.